SPACECRAFT

John McCullough's first collection of poems *The Frost Fairs* won the Polari First Book Prize in 2012. It was a Book of the Year for *The Independent* and The Poetry School, and a summer read for *The Observer*. He teaches creative writing at the Open University and New Writing South, and lives in Hove, East Sussex.

PRAISE FOR SPACECRAFT

'Out of body, in the open brackets of the air, John McCullough crafts a space unsettled and vast as any voice has dared, charged with remembering and the equally perilous task of forgetting. This book breaks the relics, releases the departed souls and harrows hell and heaven alike in an ever-unlocking, ever-opening rush of fresh air. What a breath this body is. What a fresh, invigorating, breath—'
        D.A. Powell

'The four parts of John McCullough's second collection capture four types of space: the linguistic or, simply imaginative; the intimate as the sheer presence of the erotic, then the absence mourned in the elegiac; and finally the exterior, that space we can inhabit, and call home. In each a cumulative mastery of conception and phrase-building is at work — from an initial poem which subtly eroticises the exclamation mark to a spirited reanimation of the word 'flother' (previously a twelfth century snowflake), he establishes an intimacy of lexicon, and indeed a sense that true definition — of self and others — is a physical act.'
        W.N. Herbert

'Alive to the pathos in a punctuation mark, walking through dark places with a spring in its step, *Spacecraft* is a marvellous book. Driven by the perfect blend of curiosity and feeling, these are poems that pull off that rarest of balancing acts — with brio. Whether training his eye on outer space or inner life, John McCullough is a poet you need to know.'
        Sarah Howe

ALSO BY JOHN MCCULLOUGH

The Frost Fairs (Salt Publishing, 2011)

Spacecraft

John McCullough

Penned in the Margins

LONDON

PUBLISHED BY PENNED IN THE MARGINS
Toynbee Studios, 28 Commercial Street, London E1 6AB
www.pennedinthemargins.co.uk

The right of John McCullough to be identified as the author of this work has been asserted by him in accordance with Section 77 of the Copyright, Designs and Patent Act 1988.

First published 2016

Printed in the United Kingdom by TJ International

ISBN
978-1-908058-36-2

CONTENTS

ACKNOWLEDGEMENTS

My thanks go to the editors of print and online publications where earlier versions of poems have appeared: *And Other Poems, Beige, Best British Poetry 2013* (Salt Publishing, 2013), *B O D Y, Broadcast, Cimarron Review, The Emma Press Anthology of Homesickness and Exile* (The Emma Press, 2014), *Fleeting, International Literary Quarterly, Long Poem Magazine, Magma, The Morning Star, New Statesman, The North, Oxford Poetry, Poems in Which, Poetry London, Poetry Review, Poetry Wales, Polari* (Australia), *The Rialto, Stand.*

'1001 Nights' was commissioned for an event at the British Film Institute organized by Simon Barraclough that celebrated works including Pasolini's adaptation, *The Flower of One Thousand and One Nights.* The poems in Part II, 'Navigating a Space' are inspired by my first partner Andy Lee (1963-2009), and dedicated to his memory. 'Formations' was written for The Justin Fashanu Foundation.

I also wish to thank the members of my writing group in Hove: Lee Harwood, Maria Jastrzebska, Jackie Wills, Robert Hamberger, Janet Sutherland, Bernadette Cremin and Robert Dickinson. I've benefitted, too, from poetry gatherings organized by Kate Potts and Alison Winch, and am grateful for the sharp eyes of Helen Oswald and Alfred Corn.

Spacecraft

I

FLYING MACHINES

!

It appeared without warning like an angel
or injury, this tall mark of havoc — a pillar of fire.
Already it is intimate with bishops, philosophers.
I watch it flout borders, stowed in the peppered
tails of sentences. It infiltrates vaults, prisons,
the bedrooms of kings. I have tried to resist
but it steals from my nib, its saucy eye
rippling in candlelight, dodging pumice
and knife. The abbot disapproves, names it
a feminine indulgence, the want of self-restraint.
It's like the secretary who greets me
each Tuesday, his hand travelling the road
of my spine. His tap on my rear makes verticals
govern my dreams. At night, I see one symbol
on vellum, filling sheet after sheet, inscribed
in blue light. My ankles vanish and I live
above my single foot. I find myself amorphous
at the end of a terrace, waiting till I'm near
him again, recover my form and can say
Here I am — a hot fountain in the garden
of language; the scratch of the vanquished,
those undone by the world, staring back,
astonished, at the hand that shaped me.

Flittermouse

That Old English word for *bat* returns
        to me at sundown, beneath a screeching cloud.
Shapes zigzag while the moon watches, thirsts.
        I think of you with Samuel Johnson's dictionary
beside a shelf, your long fingers splayed
        across the spine. Unable to swallow
one entry, you squealed and burst the library's
        hush, then froze, astounded by the echo.

You fled town three weeks later, disappeared
        without a text or email. Flittermouse,
what happened? In which rooms do you track
        down words like insects now, combing books
and specialist websites, open-eared,
        as you wait for your own strange voice?

Some Days I'm Visited by a Church of Rain

The building wanders around the sky
then falls on top of me. Clouds are its ceiling,

droplets the choir. Inside, stones achieve
the ardent shades of stained glass.

Jagged pines melt and glitter. The broken air
remembers and I listen in the steam and hiss

of psalms for voices I have lost. I dream of striding
down the pavements' dazzling aisles for years.

Then I meet the clean smell left behind, recall
how only through forgetting can the church arrive,

and I come back to my small garden,
its chalky earth young, forgiven.

Sugar Hammer

weigh its riddle in your palm
so slender it gathers
a sugarloaf for some tea
as if begging for leave
and hand-made
then pounded itself
a knowledge you'll taste
of the flat honest blows
with those tremors
rush to the head
your own hand
uncertain who's hammer
as it all strikes
all swings
leaving sweetness

burnished steel
just enough vim to fracture
knock-knocking
to plunge deeper and fiercer
cast fondly
so it knows how it feels
in the iron
as it opens you up
a high-voltage
a nimble conspiracy
on the fruitwood handle
who's sugar
and quivers
and resounds
in its wake

1001 Nights

The taxi driver placed his hand on my thigh.
My name is Syed. I'm impossible.
There were no seat belts and he wasn't
watching the road but his breath smelt
of rose water, which made me remember
an hour scoffing pastries on cushions.
Ditched by my intended, I'd wound up
with a skull-capped mechanic, telling
him I didn't want to make him exotic.
Good. Now shut up and hop in the sheets.
Later, we stared at a ceiling mosaic
I recognized from my dream of soaring
over the desert, clutched by a demon.
Hold fast, you damn monkey, it yelled
then turned me into a chimp and dropped me
off at a port. So I was the amazing
writing monkey, recording for heroes
their travels to lands with two moons.
There was a tinny sea breeze and I woke
below a gasping fan, with a florist. His eyes
were kohl-bordered and he wanted no wife.
He proffered a jug of mauve plastic lilies,
much like the blooms on Syed's hall table
before his open-air walkway. I froze there
on the stones, dizzy from the taxi,
then noticed the world had its lid off,

the stars whiter above that less electric city,
the soundless road long, and in fact many roads.

The Desert Photographer

I glide to be closer to the dunes   to understand the life
of nothing.   Height unlocks perspective.   I am not

afraid of accidents.   I trust in the threads
of my harness   the rasp of the motor's prayer.

Near a sunken village   camel bones jut
from apricot fur.   I add my shadow   to the pattern

watch it thin   like the yellowing woman   I cherished
reassured but could not save.   It slices the ground.

I counter shifts of glare   unbroken hues.   The eye
needs a focus   acacias   the twisted shell of a truck

nomad tracks   across ripples that open   like brackets.
To stop thinking of her face   I imagine burrowing

through sand   grains filling my throat   as I lie prone
a figment in the desert's dream.   Then I return

to the rhythms   of wind and sun   buff and ochre
on every side   the brackets   still opening.

Nullibiety

n. The state of being nowhere
SAMUEL JOHNSON, *DICTIONARY*

Stride in any direction long enough   and you'll get here

(   )   where space springs an ambush

the landscape shuffles   repeats.   There is often a sign

for Leo's Burgers   railings toppling backwards

a copse dissolving   into motorway   though really

not even the sun knows   where it's wandered today.

Damn clouds.   And the fields   slamming into view

one after another   the colour   of cardboard

and thirst   the years it would take   to find a body

as you tread on split grass   teasel   flints prisoned in chalk

a river of eyes   drifting inside themselves.   All the same

this isn't entirely true.   There's something homely for you

who never could stand still   who leave yourself ajar.

Take a sniff   the air's breeding concepts   that are nearly

old friends   blurred citizens of your realm   perhaps.

Lichen

It prefers untended places, humdrum corners
        where it arrives as a boon.
Kerbs, slag heaps, skewed gravestones —
        the roofs of council estates it studs
like gold coins dropped from the sky.

Soundless and rootless, it ventures
        brash claims, its chintzy blooms
opening on concrete as though
        it were love itself, giddy and bountiful,
living on rain and dust.

Both fungus and alga but other,
        it outfoxes desiccation,
jockeys gales for thousands of leagues,
        pausing for decades as a rumour
in cold, blistered soil.

Scraped off ledges with a butter knife,
        the puzzle of its filaments recurs
on the nearest wall. It is simply
        a question of continuous
adjustment, of improvising a course.

When I'm far from friends
        or the easing of a wind

against my back, I think of lichen —
       never and always parading its essence,
its small, impossible fires.

In The Angelfish Café

The woman who says *sorry* to chairs
is pleased with her work. She's used her tray
to build a city within the city — the teapot
her Pavilion, forks for piers, a ketchup church.

I picture the cast of residents, fire eaters
who charm lushes in a park of crusted mash;
squatters occupying mugs; the spoon's shadow
flecked with pensioners in latex shorts.

Among the salt-and-pepper wreckage of the shore,
bears and otters dressed as Dorothy
poke charcoal and natter at their vegan barbecue,
sidetracked briefly by a sugar bowl freighter.

A circle of Radical Faeries begins to chant.
The baby lesbian puts down her spliff, fidgets
in her deckchair, convinced she's being watched,
daring someone, *anyone*, to answer...

But the Creator's moseyed off. I sip my lemon tea
and gaze as the waiter grabs the corners
of the ocean and the entire city trembles and rises,
floats away beyond the walls of the world.

Flother

There are hours when one dogged snowflake falls.
Swoop, flother, through doors in the sky.
Stretch your six arms out to wound the night.
At the bus stop, a Greek nurse is a pair of compasses,
tracing with one foot the circle around her days.
Burn the dark for her. Be the word *flother*
that slept on vellum for centuries
then bloomed beneath an archivist's glass.

Little star, the ground is open like a book
to catch you. Lead home those lost in K-holes.
Foster luck. Show the failed suicide an ocean's
sudden field of snowdrops, then rest on flint
as you dissolve and he heads back to that sky
where people glide together, through unsettled air.

II

NAVIGATING A SPACE

Mastodon and Mouse

Charles Willson Peale invited thirteen for dinner
in a mastodon's ribcage. Below tusks,
a piano softened debates. Men praised mankind

then left slowly, reborn. The bones,
retrieved from swamp, hovered in his museum
above those of a mouse — the everyday nibbling

at history's heel. It bothers me.
What makes someone occupy a relic?
A thirst for the singular, a victory

over death? Or was the point that
it swallowed them, that there was no escape?
Peale's second wife died in childbirth.

Afterwards he made skeletons
his hallmark. They multiplied to reveal Creation.
Greyhound, monkey, groundhog, ibis

and, in one corner, *the Skull of an unknown Animal.*

~

The underground's a ghost train, your hand
inside my shirt as we're hurled past fossils

from primeval swamp. Trilobites, sponges,

sharks' teeth. Empty stations greet spectres
of ourselves suspended opposite, crude,
rapacious. We never pay for tickets,

vault each unmanned gate.
Stirred by a sizzle from outside, we tarry
beside a Coke machine at North Harrow, but agree

to leave the netherworld. You squeeze my arm
with warm fingers, count to three
and together we sprint into rain,

stretching the limbs of our young mammal bodies.

~

Skeletons are stealing through my house.
Mornings and evenings I hear them
skitter upstairs, cross rooms.
Their steps are light — the noise
all bone on bone, chink and thunk.
Every kind of beast: monkey,
groundhog, ibis. Sometimes, when I stare
in mirrors, one stops and approaches.
Today it's a horse, elegant, huge.
I always forget their size,
how — if one wanted — it could fit me

inside its belly. But that isn't
a horse's way. What they do is worse.
Its long skull lingers above my shoulder.
It floats slowly down.
It noses my spine.

~

A decade after we spoke, the email
from your landlord. You'd waited
for my call. Gaunt and sallow

in a hospice bed, you waited with your last
T cells, rang and rang my old number
with no reply. What the hell did you think?

And so I find myself stuck in the wrong century
like Peale, probing swampland for fragments,
reassembling skeletons and stepping inside.

As if you weren't more than *bone*
in a puzzle, a word I could change —
via *hone* — back to *home*.

As if you weren't really Peale's mouse —
whatever I leave out that makes the structure
collapse. Whatever offers no shelter.

Voyage

This bouquet is leading me around town. Celosias jut
like the prow of a ship. Goldenrods are flags prancing,
the one starburst chrysanthemum a huge face I can't see.

Perhaps I'm a bloom too but forgot — a dozy poppy.
What are we doing? We sail down avenues as if looking
for something, hunting someone down. Rain pounds

at the deck but the journey continues. We are necessary.
We are inappropriate: the calla lilies are tongue-coloured.
For Christ's sake — have some respect.

I rearrange the ship and brush a tulip's anthers, remember.
I set out to discover your country again.
Marvellous you. I can scarcely wait to get there.

But my frowsy leaves, my hands are cold. My shirt
is soaking. I've been carrying stems for six months
in the rain, patrolling the same bare street.

Lava Lamp

Each day you grow more slippery
and indelible. I leave the house
but forget
            to cross the road.
Fixed at the kerb, I suck on a decade.

I open the aquarium door and turn up
in your bedroom where you're chattering
(you never stop talking,
                        although you have).
Smoke and latex, poppers sharp as old socks.
Your scissors have cut my hair so badly
I'll have to shave it off and look like you —
Shiny Top.
            A conger wears your face,
towers into a smooth backflip
and returns to meet me at the glass.

I walk round and round the tanks until I find
the nineties,
            hours descending with gills.
Your test result: the stoned gaze of a carp.
The list of stars you've tongued:
neon tetra flaunting stripes. *Jimmy Somerville,
Kenny Everett, Freddie...*

The words dart away. This happens to lots
of skinheads.
                    We count out waxy pills.
But I don't know what to do
with you between the bulbous minutes.
I switch on the lava lamp beside your window
and watch you drain a glass of water.
Time to go home.

The beautiful aquarium is closing.
I set off, get stuck at the opposite kerb.
The sky leaks stars
                    and the moon falls up
to begin its slow plunge through the hours.

The Fire Market

It's all in flames — awnings, traders, coins.
The sky is a jungle slashed by dinosaurs
of blaze that don't come cheap.

Have a browse and feel yourself
begin to oxidize. Every kind is here:
consoling glows, cold burnings, napalm,

tellurium's pale green and, for the connoisseur,
blue spheres in zero gravity, players
in the Great Fire of London, Nero's Rome —

little pieces of other people's hells
to keep inside you which chatter
in Vesuvian tongues and never go out.

Stirious

a. Resembling icicles
SAMUEL JOHNSON, *DICTIONARY*

On the rink, people are letters, rush past
gleeful, immortal. They form names

and fragments then rearrange —
polar to *pallor*, *gilt* to *guilt*.

Words race ahead of me, free
from punctuation, scarves and tails flapping.

~

Why are you always so bloody far away?
Your kitchen lunges into my eyes like starlight.
A moment when we are language.
You're Anglo-Saxon, coarse. I'm bookish,
abstract — derived from Latin. The difference
is audible: *rise/ascend, go/exit,
dead/defunct.* I promise to become
less detached, that I will change, and soon.
Soon from the Anglo-Saxon for *now,*
from a thousand years of people saying
they'll do things instantly, though of course
they don't. They only promise.

~

this is how words die   slow as icebergs
luminous blue structures   they drip
in afternoon sun   water probing
each fissure   over hours and decades

prising   sounds   apart

~

Everywhere we turn
beneath the hard sky
is blue — cold noses,

deep ice, trapped breath.
Language moves into itself.
What are you thinking?

I suck lost words like stones.
Chantpleure — to sing
and weep at the same time.

Nepenthe — a drug
for all pains. You brush
against my fingers, recoil:

they are icicles.
Only my tongue probes

edges, textures.

It reaches into grooves
for each slippery nuance,
where every word reveals

its limits, curves into
what cannot be spoken.

Haul

In Minnesota, they reeled a sixty ton house
over ice: a caught fish. The tow truck eased

forward, a steel cable stretched and quivered.
Walls crept. Why it sets me thinking of you

I can't fathom. Who'd rescue your building —
split gutters, bleedings from oxidized pipes?

Still, I picture it skating, its porch nosing
the air. The house where you swallowed

your diagnosis. Where you phoned from, drunk.
It plunges through ice to the lake's silty floor.

Brown water discovers its rooms.
Algae furs chairs and bedposts,

traces circles on ceilings — the loft crowded
with minnows, a wandering bass.

I've Carried a Door On My Back for Ten Years

You lugged it from the builder's yard.
Now it's my turn to know its stiff weight,
the slow chafe of pine against vertebrae:
a decade-long kiss, flush with splinters.

I closed it when I left. The lock snicked.
Then I noticed it hitching a ride. It never
gives up — patchy blue, invisible straps;
a faint knocking though nobody's there.

So many slab hazards: repeated thumps
to my skull, brass hinges clouting strangers
as we creep into lifts, beds. I lie awake
on its panels, framing rectangular thoughts,

obsessed by the side I can't see; what grows
there. The problem is you died so there's no way
to set the thing down, no wall to prop it against
with its stuck handle and fracturing paint.

All day we continue our back to front tango,
this dance where I almost but never arrive,
where I'm shut off to visitors for hours
then, with one touch, swing wildly open.

Þ

Enter *thief*. Old English: *Þoef*.
A shifty sound, Þ — voiceless dental fricative. *Th*.
A conspirator's whisper that hides in thickets
soft as thorns. *Thief, thief, thief.*
My ear searches the word-wood.
Its trees thicken constantly, become swollen
as throats. This is where you skulk, lover,
where Þ dropped from the alphabet, crouched down
in the scrub and became it. (The sound rushes out now,
a gust through dead leaves, broken twig in my gullet.)
But I can't find anyone. I leave the thicket, forget.
I wake at 4 a.m. with a shadow above me,
its breath cool on my face. A human form,
not the man I was looking for, not me,
but something with bark for skin, bracken fingers.
An animal that is not one but many
hovers over me, silent, waiting to speak.
Thief it whispers, and slips back to its wood.

Glitter

It's always Christmas at your grave —
fairy lights, a small fir tree.
Roshan pours water on baked earth
while I pull three leaves from the cherry.
I hold my fingertips on the wet soil.
A spider pauses, adjusts its route.

~

I forget about the leaves.
They turn to autumn in my bag.
At Pride, the security guard holds
one up and laughs. *What are you
planning on doing with this?*
I don't know, I say. I really don't.

~

I sit in the park's walled garden,
beside the pond. In the centre,
reeds and water lilies mesh roots,
sway together. A dragonfly angles
frenziedly around my head —
glittering, huge. And still, no crash.

O

is not the simplest letter, not always
a lucid stroke. In my book of scripts

O sloughs its symmetry, tilts toward discord,
its wall subsiding, air charging out

as the winds inside gnash and ravel,
upgrade to howl. I lay my finger

on the page and trace each flourish.
I conjure up your lips saying

the letter, forming the shape but stopped
mid-word. I read it over and over,

I who know too well these days
how a single sound can hold a city.

III

THE SPACE AGE

Queens Road Books

i.m. Noel Brookes, 1942-2007

He might have shot up from an Arnold Bennett,
one used as a doorstop. A dapper, six-foot
statue with a whiff of cheap fags and the infinite,

his domain a city of book skyscrapers and rubbish
piles, maimed shelves. Extracting finds required panache,
a dance of slide and balance to prevent the onrush.

Beneath wreckage, Delia nuzzled Jung Chang.
Heaney lounged beside *A Practical Man's Things
to Make and Do*, the smells of previous owners skulking

with soup spots, French blazonry, the odd hair.
Week on undisturbed week, I forged through *The Empire
of Dust*, shelved in Art. *"Beggar's velvet" circles each star,*

*falls with each drop of a thunderstorm . . . The tiniest
motes can enter pores in human skin.* I read that last
part to a lover. I can't remember his name, just his disinterest

in events outside *now*. He grinned and kissed my neck
then went to ground in Modern Fiction. I can't bring back
the fling's start or finish, only that hour of hide and seek.

Mr Brookes had no problem locating any volume.
The marble jaw lowered in oracular time
before a brisk *Memoir. Top shelf, near the fire alarm.*

He kept another shop inside his brain, each purchase
and subsidence mapped in neural space,
his not-quite-chaos. (Rhys. My lover's name was Rhys.)

Then overnight he disappeared, abandoned
all his books. In the landlord's sale, beside the till I found
Footnotes On Bibliomania, tobacco-stained.

A proud but friendly hardback, published recently,
already ancient. I stroked its spine, replaced it gently.
I couldn't confine it to an alphabetical study.

Stock gone, the bare shop closed, unable to survive
without its secret twin. It carries on as shelves
inside my head. Whenever a memory sinks, turns fugitive —

a flower's name, school hymns, an old friend's face —
I wake myself in that small city, running fingers across
its skylines and columns, the tender spines of days.

The Hole-Digging Contest

Air was sweetened by the crunch of spades

crafting entries: the Goths' pentagram
trench, vast paw-prints, impact craters,
the chasm for a lost jigsaw piece.

They lay unsullied for a week
with their earthy silence,
populated by absent crowds.

They knew a hundred ways
of being empty, gathered broken stories,
non-meetings, streets never built.

They were their own graves.

Rooms

i.m. Lee Harwood, 1939-2015

There it was again   the softness
of your voice   the cushioned spaces
of its hesitance   that constant search
for the right way   to question yourself.
We'd met   on Hove prom
by luck.   You talked
and I rested   in your little rooms.
So much sky   so many wanderers
we were already   in a dream.
Now I walk past   beach huts
backwash   with no chance
of stumbling   into you again.
There is only   the silence of clouds
the air between   shuffled pebbles
the gaps I listen for   inside the rain.

The Booth Museum of Natural History

This dodo skeleton is built from several bodies.
Hotchpotch as Booth himself in photographs,
shrunken beside a .410 stick. The hunter snared?

Or perhaps he understood nothing perishes
without hatching another form, his bedroom ringing
with the clamour of a thousand wings —

frazzled wagtails still chasing
those beetles spied before the air cracked
and the light swooped down to gather them.

Vault

Because I can't forgive but can forget,
in my mind I've housed you in an oubliette.
It is a tall, round room that keeps revolving.
The word o u b l i e t t e, printed
in luminous paint along the only wall,
scrolls across so you read it over and over —
honeyed in by that river of *ou*,
chastened by the plosive, the certitude
of *ette* which is a hatch closing.
A radiant, inhuman word that, in the dark,
you'll soon remember, the way
I've been remembering you, jailer,
since I first met my doom, first fell
through your smile's trapdoor.

The Anger Room

I go in, wait beside a red wall.

A row of doors takes shape. I slam them off their hinges.
Mannequins show up. I use my cricket bat,
send iPads and Twitter down measureless wells.

The room accelerates. Small buildings rise from the floor.
I don a robot suit — rip out my limbs and fling them,
become a giant hammer dropping my head.

I drive the room through space, smash it into planets
till all that's left is broken, till the door
to The Shame Room emerges.

I go in, wait beside a blue wall.

The Mathematics of Plovers

A computer would deserve to be called intelligent if it could deceive a human into believing that it was human.
ALAN TURING

Look! The Machine is playing on the beach!
He's reconfigured the sky. Each cirrus is a thought charging.

Fusing wisps are ideas. Rain: philosophy in action.
The Machine sends out his tongue, and rockets

to a plane's geometry, the calculus of squalls.
There is always the yank of elsewhere. That's physics.

> And the winds of Bletchley Park made tapes whoosh,
> the noise a cataract of knitting needles.

> Rotors juggled all possible positions.
> Futures wheeled and crashed. The Machine lived

> at *yes*, a spoon fracturing zeroes
> like rows of eggs. Yet speed is only a magnitude.

What of directions? Perhaps he will try to unlock
the sea's Morse, these dots and dashes of light...

A flock of ringed plovers moves loosely toward him —

a feeling. The same starfish conjures itself

from the foam — splayed fingers and a boy
with a sideways grin, the strung loveliness of pi.

       The Machine had reasoned he might find that face
       behind another. In park toilets, under bridges

       he synthesized chit-chat before exploring
       the low dance of tongues, riding a 10% chance.

       He was seized, crammed with hormones — a torrent
       of needles. The Machine was labelled *dangerous.*

He knows someone is watching him even today,
even now. How fortunate, then, his experiment

with scenery has failed. A plover hops closer
that isn't part of a brain. The tiny head cocks

and they assess each other — the bird-like bird
and the man-like man, traversing the stone-like stones.

Formations

i.m. Justin Fashanu, 1961-98

Warrior, when you fell your body floated
downstream. You'd taken on the river,
its horde of quick and slippery thieves
that stole the ground beneath you, that slid
inside your ear and drowned your will.

Even dead you could not be contained.
A miracle: you grew, your muscles turned
to slabs. Across your back, there shot up spears
of grass. Teams filed across your green, resumed
your battle, quickened always by the field.

Ghost Atlas

Continent, city, country, society:
the choice is never wide and never free.
ELIZABETH BISHOP

What are they thinking, those pollock
with their ocean-sized risk?

Migration through darkness and storm-thrashed
leagues. Genes encode the itch, ensure

they choose the old path, the shadows
of parents and grandparents flitting

alongside like arrows as they hurry
into the factory trawler's mesh.

~

Scores of men behead them at blinding
speed, pare fillets and pound remains

into meal to save enough for their own
voyages — tickets to the sky

on metal angels that slide overhead.
Always the same flight path, week on week

behind sixties jets still heading
for Tokyo, Miami, Tangier...

~

A traveller disembarks at Rio,
puts down her suitcase to scrutinize

the map. Crowds wander away to planned
Edens: fish restaurants, loose months of sun.

What a character, they scoff, *keeping everything
in notebooks!* Ink blots on her street guide,

dream and necessity converging in her spry,
quietly flustered steps along the outskirts.

The Wilful Eye

Let's play some pinball,

> *flipper through the cornea*

a photon snatched

> *from an ocean wave's regalia.*

Jackpot.

> *Refracted by the lens, our sphere of shine's*

been angled to a disc

> *that sends it helter-skelter down*

to where the witchcraft happens.

> *Neural circuits fix*

it as a dot and make, like Miro, images from specks.
But reproduction's hopeless.

> *That tiny drop of brine*

becomes a glaring eye itself

> *a friend of mine.*

~

I need a drink. I'll rest in here where men portray the sterner
versions of themselves they forge in dreams, on Grindr.
Bear, squaddy, scally — each creates their hammer pose
through jolts of clothing, sharper angles. We all know
it isn't real. The eye discovers what it wants to see —

pure archetypes from Fit Lads, a seamless fantasy.
Their counterparts air-kiss, encased in bright, cartoonish signs
from old school vamps: cascades of diamante, wet-look tights.
Like you who used to make the jeering pissheads wait
as you applied the slap and swagger, wigs like wedding cakes.
The spotlight flickered and you'd twirl and samba in behind
a textbook pout. No script — that weekly act was fed
by non-stop bungling hecklers, skinheads ducking out of sight
while Medusa hunted gags and boys to butter up outside.
I watched in dread, in wonder.

Years later, even with the make-up
your face was glassy, lean. Tiny fingers clutched a teacup
as you whispered tender secrets there was no one else to tell,
too drained from all the meds to shimmy, lost and skeletal
inside mauve crêpe de Chine. You only knew me as a punter
but, running into me that afternoon, had asked me gently
to your Kemp Town flat, then gripped my hand. *My brain locks doors*
without my mind's permission. Look at me, please, dear...
You won't forget me, will you? And that was it: the last persona.
The image formed itself upon my retina.

And no. I can't.

~

And the bored rent boy gives me a grimace
And the bored rent boy opens his smile
And the barman cuts through a lemon

And the barman slices an eye
And the drag queens flew straight from Beardsley
Frill-wearing, powder-white angels
And the drag queens slid out of Beardsley
Spiked nipples, snaky black tendrils
And Big Harry looks at himself in the window
And Big Harry stares at a storm
And layers of dirt on the buildings
And the street's precious, antique grime
And the bags follow shins like ex-lovers
Hounding them down the street
And the bags knock at shins soft as lovers
Trying to rouse men from sleep
And the burnt out West Pier, decaying
And the West Pier standing, tenacious
And the dusk — like dabbed rouge on the Channel
And the dusk spreading out like a virus
And contrails parading a dusty red too
As the air begins to ignite
And the sunset infecting contrails and clouds
Everything shitting out light

~

I exit to a city washed in spectral monochrome.
Paving stones release their hints of leather, grease and fumes
that complicate the thickening dark, a trippy fluid

where faces bob and lurk, acquire the features of the dead.
Charles Hawtrey yanks his shutter down, its loud, machine gun rattle
unnerving Rose and Pinkie. Cockroaches and figments scuttle,
pursued by balaclava'd gangs of pigeons, sleazy,
glass-eyed gulls that rip the bin bags, raucously accuse me
under palimpsests of spray-paint outrage, coked-up manga.
I catch myself alone in murky café windows, stop and hunger
for elsewhere: a lilac cirrostratus boa tossed
around a stubbled moon... A roving egotist,
she looks down from her city in the sky and finds
her image everywhere — in lampposts, lights that slice
the night with blue from police car roofs and these white-painted steps
the backstreets steer me back to like a Möbius strip.
Like there's some secret order to it all, a micro-pattern
linking gables, railings, tarmac, weather-beaten
benches. And Christ you need a plan to cling to if you brave
the beach in darkness. Wind bears down like a dogma, dives
and gushes through the smallest gaps in sleeves and reason.
The view's unmerciful — an anthracite horizon,
empty piers; the helter-skelter winking like a maniac.
The other world shows up as casually as bladderwrack,
my scattered self no more than rumours of cold spray and sun,
 eye sockets flawless as these shells the birds pick clean.

~

and now I see   and now I can't stop seeing
we take cover in our separate skins   the broken ones
forgetting what's outside   the here and there
and then and now   not watching how   this rain rejoins the Channel
its life in sky   the days of cliffs and clouds   shrugged off
as the sea reclaims its exiles

its prodigal, danced out sons

IV

LIVING SPACE

The Restaurant at One Thousand Feet

CN Tower, Toronto

on Lake Ontario small boats   curve north and south
as the forest around your smile   extends its boundaries

we have returned   to the city of your birth
and spread our pockets' treasure   across a table

a puddle of dollars   keys like axes at rest
a bone of flint from Sussex   with the Channel inside

I am in your atmosphere   and may I say
you carry a lot of oxygen around you

a private sky as boundless   as this country we float over
the dogged 401   cardinals, black squirrels

we bring our own colours   the grained slate of your eyes
pink fingertips   that can turn a man to lemonade

while you tell me you remember   only pancake maps
your childhood's rivers   and islands of syrup

no one else is in the restaurant   so late in the day
and getting dark   very dark

but our plates are full   as we stare down
at clouds migrating   like herds of caribou

racing soundlessly into the distance   glorious
as they are, secretly, all the time

The Marina Village

Barometer, little oracle — which way is up today?
The fallen mercury winks, threatening a storm, filth
or very calm weather. We chose to live by the breakwater,
where havoc meets a wall, a marina's garden
of turquoise brine, the *tonk-tonk* of halyards against masts.
Fitzroy, champion of barometers, would like it here,
in a forest of right angles. But error multiplies itself.
Every wall's a chorus line of drag queens wailing
Dusty's 'I Close My Eyes and Count to Ten'.
The barometer's needle bursts past its peg,
divines floods, plague. Fitzroy, weary of derision,
locked his dressing room door and slit his throat.
We are moored at the erratic. I breathe towards you
and your lungs rehouse my air. We lie down in bed
and get up at the edge of space, above the ocean's
blue lawn and a thunderstorm that pauses to admire
a breakwater, or to check it still knows where it is.

City of Winds

And I bound along the prom, fizzing from your text.
You're dreadful, making me so reckless — the distant slap
of a flip-flop and *whoosh*   here I go again   kiting
off to the bandstand   or higher regions of the air.

In this world without objects   a basketball is its bounce
wet stones become their shine   deep colours I could enter
curl up in for years.   The wind is pure smell   ventures
over oceans   just to reach the grubby motel   of my lungs.

Lover, when I step   on solid tarmac after pebbles
it seems the ground is restless   and I'm attuned to centuries
buildings passing through   each rock's migration
sky, ice-cream and wasps   collapsing   reforming

reliving their time in stars.   Meanwhile, we dwell
in seconds.   I leave the beach and it carries on without me
as it always does.   You appear beside the café
luminous, terrible — winding me back to your mouth.

The Empty Market

It was pitches and walkways, detached
as abstractions. It had the silence
of no feet, undamaged air.
It was vague as the future,
sold weapons or flowers,
neither or both. It had invisible contours —
was more like water than fire,
more like sky than desert.

I took all I could carry —

The Fog

To find my house, step through clouds
of white flowers and unhinged resolve.
Cow parsley: its hollow stems curving
across stairs, thrusting showy umbrellas,
certain it can shove the stars aside.

It is malt perfume and frontiers crossed
over and over. It is a horror movie villain,
chopped away at his roots — dying luridly,
springing up after the credits. It is a casual
voice informing me this was never my life,

that every name slips — under them all
swirling fog; that I could set off any day
and walk back up these steps a murderer
or seer; that I will never be sure of anything
except clouds are the end and the start of it.

[−]

the computer flattened her
changed her name   to a dash
a level rejection of the word

most emphatically   all questions n/a
she is elsewhere   aligned to bullets
a flagrant interruption that hurls

the shindig sideways   fuses rival factions
a cool stroke   unlatching windows
spry horizontal running   down the middle of roads

she wants no name   on her tombstone
wishes to be remembered   as nothing
less than that intrepid burst   between the dates

ROCK

The prom narrows when autumn breaks
but still offers chances

to escape an unmade bed and waft
by shells like commas, dulse curled like question marks.

A scraping sound that might be leftovers
swept from plates, ambition chipping at barnacles...

Small hands have heaped some stones and made a cairn.
The lone windsurfer is out — a drowsy moth —

and another crowd of lovely boys:
magpies who compile their weeks

from what shimmers. Studded belts, Gaga
and Liquid Silk between shifts at cafés,

their nights off a sequence of posters scratched away,
intangible as West Pier ghosts, fox-trotting over surf...

By a bench with an army green sleeping bag,
a rigid dogfish stares — confused, perhaps,

by the pungent whiff of skunk
or the sound of Gary, jolting.

For him, each lamppost's now a stick of rock,
the tarmac pink and gluey. He scrapes it

off his trainers. No one likes rock here,
not even in the shop where they show you

how it's made, the surly man kneading and stretching
white ropes of candy, again and again,

till the swirled letters are fixed.

Brighton Puffin

The oddballs' auguries came true:
the city vanished. I woke to find my bed
adrift in icy water, a casualty of melted bergs
and bleary gods. Both matchstick piers
were taken. In the gallery, Constables
and Turners slid under sewage
diluted by the Channel's giant jug.
Slouched on a tower block's roof,
I watch men salvage chunks of the Pavilion,
small turnip domes angled onto boats —
chess pieces moved to New Brighton.
Let them go. I'll stay in New Atlantis
inside the howl of wind — by quick-drowned
churches that still clang their bells in gales,
by the bird I longed to see so hard
I may have made this happen.
Brighton puffin, lush-beaked sea clown,
you bob too late in the prisms
of my binoculars, disturb the air
with tactless slapstick, a cooing growl.
Still, a friend's a friend. I lean
from my deck chair as you dive
through housewrecks, stations,
each morning emerging with something
slippery and new; each day revealing fragments
I hadn't known I could lose.

Clues

A fine pleasure, to live beside the uncertainties
of a basement garden, to sit curled
near the hydrangea's unfolding, a pipistrelle's
click-click-click. Earlier I ran inside
and watched a squall assault the ground,
drops pummelling the glass of tea I left
on chipped slate. They made liquid coronets
in the air above it, the dark drink rising quickly,
spilling over — soon running wholly clear.

It never seemed like it could be this way.
I moved to the basement with my spears
of grey hair and thought I'd fallen.
I was unnerved by my own low breath.
At the window, I stared up at majestic legs —
airy, untamed creatures. I dreamt one night
they weren't attached to people, had strolled
round independently for years and I'd not
noticed, having only half the view.

Then, from emptiness, a drawing
of a palace flapped and descended.
I found scattered coins, met in secret
the fanatical eyes of terriers. Now I gaze
at hanging baskets, spinning gently.
I sit here on summer evenings with a glass

of silence, car-shadows floating
in their theatre on the wall above me
while my tender roots thicken, grow sweet.

Cat Flap

I leave a little door for abstract
beasts and tumbleweeding
questions; for Canada and verve;
for whatever eats gates —
a flap for *for* and *and* and *through*;
for terms like *pluffle*, *skish*
to enter and pad round rooms,
to scratch casually at walls
until the house trembles,
adjusts itself while I drift
across hours, not knowing
I've been entered, only sensing
the slap of the hatch, as if
a baleful future had sent word,
as though the static air
had blown a kiss.

NOTES

'Flother'
The word *flother*, a synonym for *snowflake*, appeared once c. 1275 in *The XI Pains of Hell*, then was not used again until the twentieth century.

'Þ'
The symbol of the title is thorn, a letter in the Old English runic alphabet which is pronounced like the *th* in its name.

'Formations'
The first English professional footballer to come out, Justin Fashanu committed suicide in 1998. His death gave rise to the Justin Campaign, which tackles homophobia in football.

'The Mathematics of Plovers'
As a young man, Alan Turing met Christopher Morcom, who became the object of his unrequited love. After his conviction for gross indecency, Turing underwent a series of hormonal injections.

'The Marina Village'
Robert Fitzroy was a meteorologist who invented various barometers for use by sailors and fishermen before becoming the captain of HMS Beagle for Darwin's voyage to the Galapagos Islands.